SACRED WORDS

LET MY WORDS HEAL YOU

PRANJAL GOSAI

ISBN 979-888555585-2

The book is dedicated to the people who inspired me to write but
will not read a single phrase.
I have been a person of art. What truly inspired me to write poems
is an incident that happened
in grade fourth.
Its quite amusing that a child who gets first price in poem
competition starts writing poems
on subjects she never explored. All i did was reading. Reading
poetry and copying the style of
writing is all i did untill i got my hands on it.
Life experiences and phases intimated the long lost poet in my
subconscious mind. And
that's how i jumped into writing this book. This is my first ever
book of Poetry. There might be
unpolished work but i would want to say this to the reader that
you surely will feel connected to
my words.

Contents

Preface

It gives me immense pleasure to publish my first ever book of poetry. This book is a collection
of poems on love, frolics and romances and hard to swallow phrases of melancholy and grief.
As a child i always wanted to write my feelings ,draw my emotions into little poems . Back in
2020 when the world was facing pandemic , my leisure intimated that long lost poet to write
again and thats how this book took birth.
I am thankful to the publishing platform for providing me who is an unpolished poet a chance to
self publish my book.
I will be forever grateful for the same.

Acknowledgements

The life has been a roller coaster since adolescence. It will continue to be the same though i
am grateful for the temporary and permanent ones in my life. The work of art here is all done
because of your presence and absence in my life.

First Words

I have been living a life of rules
No wonder why
The zeal to be perfect halted my drools
I breath behold and believe
Had an idea that i shall relieve
One fine night..
I was into a fight
I popper with a sound and went clueless with the wound
I saw the words, I felt the words
The words that break me, the words that shake me
The words that impart me tears
Only i can paddle up my gears..

Mine

My precious pearl
My lunar for whom i am lunatic
Its just so fantastic
My morning star my prettiest scar
Strings to my broken guitar
How i want to hold you
Like a child holds its candy jar
My forever desire
You set my soul to fire
Come to me my sweetest prayer
You are the one i will keep up to stare
Run into my veins emerge into me
Like the almighty we never share

I Will Make You Smile

When you feel down
When you drop your crown
When your days seem harder
Everything full for you is quarter
I promise i will make you smile
Though i am away from you miles
I will make your days better and nights bright
Keep yourself in my arms right
I will make you calm and light
I know i am crazy sometimes and breezy always
But babe, you have been in pain for a while
Come to me
I will make you smile

Meet

When we meet
I will make the galaxy shine bright
We stargaze side by side
You are my moon
My shine, my little secret
I will forever hide
I won't let you fall
I will hold you tight
When we meet
The birds will sing, the angels
Will shower the blossoms they bring
The days with be golden and
Starry will be the nights.

Hundred Springs

I hope i see hundred springs with you
With my eyes closed
I will see through your eyes
Aren't they mine too?
I hope all the tears i shed
I shed on your shoulders
We walk hand in hand
Through grasses and boulders
You defined me a different forever
The second i see you to the second i can't
You have me into parts
No mortals can tear us apart

Beautiful

I saw a dangling heart
I saw subtle lips
I saw devastating smile, i saw a bright cherry
So bright as a berry
World defines it incorrectly
To me the lips,the smile
The flaws seen far from a mile..
The expression so thoughtful
The blush so cheerful
"Ugly" may be to the world
To me he is beautiful

In Love

They both crazy
They both in love
They flew high like a pair of dove
In the era of hate and war
They reached wonder shore
They shared smiles and tears they shared
Walked on stoned paths "what pain?"
They never cared
They enjoyed struggles
Romances for them were hurdles
They both crazy
They both in love

Home

I got air , i got smiles in my share
I can almost see through the darkness
If you knew how much this means to me
If you knew how happy you are making me
And how i crave your touch so much
That
It feels like home to me
Feels like i am all the way back
Where i belong
I want to keep you stuck forever
Along
Because it feels like home to me

Tried

I am not a winner for sure
But my intentions were pure
I couldn't give you all what you deserve
But my life , darling i put to serve
I tried.. tried harder
I had dreams to create wonder
Kept myself there for you
Always and forever .

I Wish

He knew I was going
Did not ask me to hold on
Though his knowing
I shed tears , he knew my fears
I was into fright
All alone that night
I am no a soldier
Nor a human of power
I melt down when loved and sob when pain you shower
No wonder he has my heart
But only he tears me apart
I wish he mends me
I wish he bends me
And holds me tight
Hugs me more and loves me throughout all lonely nights

You

When had days darker
When had times harder
When i was thrifted
Bitter has the experience felt
My eyes usually never melt
Broke to you and it melted
Ain't no one could hold on
Ain't no one could shower all of it
Its you who brings it on
And makes me glow with every part of it

Forever

We were meant to be forever
It happened never
Its not the end my dear
We may never meet but surely crossed paths
How can i forget the moment we hath..
Keeping all the memories in my heart
The last salute of love i impart

Dreams

I have my dreams
Carried by my wings..
Far far away , down the clouds
The stars that bling
The ballad of my victory
Together they sing..
One day the folks shall see
I will be who i want to be
Alone i will arise
No sorrow no demise

Void

I feel a void
I feel hollow, sheer emptiness
The vaccum in life
I don't know where my paths go
I don't know when I was embraced in love
Ahh! Years ago
Is this the adulting they talked about
Is this the life they cried aloud
I want to go back in time
To cure my wounds

Late

They say I am always late
Late to talk, late to walk, late to utter,
I wonder and later i regret..
I believe all the things you crave are not always in your fate..
But sure i go on and ask lord, all the happiness that they let..
They say hope is god
And i am the even in all odds..
Surpassing all the grudges I behold
I have heard my favorite quote
"Good things come to those who wait"
So its better to be late

Broken Wings

How much ever I try
I couldn't fly.
Why are my wings broken,torn and bruised
Am i cursed or the problem is the way
I am raised
My eyes have seen the darkest clouds and the deepest seas
All my power .. the devils of world ,
Seize
I shut them close
So no thorns can be a rose..

Failed

There was a shadow..
That followed me in my sorrow..
When my feet shook..
The concominant i forrow..
He was the shoulder on which i cried..
Maybe I failed to love ..
But atleast I tried..

Wait

I don't know if I am in love...
But damn.... when you call my name out..
My heart pops out..
When you look into my eyes..
And call me cute..
My mind dances and my soul plays flute..
I don't know if i am in love..
But ..when you ask me to sing your favorite song..
Ahhhh i have been waiting for this since long...

Prayers And Wishes

You are in my prayers and wishes
I know you are the one that pulls my heart and seizes
Could you be more closer
A bit nearer
Around me like a wasp to a flower
Babe you are, yes you are
In my prayers and wishes
We stay together , forever
In no time we have been for each other.

Last Salute

I was lying
Weak and tired
All night crying..wondering why all this happened
My eyes so red and sunken
I wish i could have hugged you a little more longer
A bit more firm and stronger
The truth cannot be denied
The fact that you lied
All the promises
The unforgotten kisses
Will remain close to my heart
The Last salute of love i impart.

9 798885 555852

Printed by Libri Plureos GmbH in Hamburg, Germany